Bicester
In Camera

by Michael J. Morgan LMPA LBIPP

QUOTES LIMITED of BUCKINGHAM

MCMLXXXVI

Published by Quotes Limited
Buckingham, England in 1986
and in this second impression in 1990

Typeset in Plantin by
Key Composition of Northampton, England

Pictures Lithographed by
South Midlands Lithoplates Limited, Luton, England

Printed by Busiprint Limited
Buckingham, England

Bound by J. W. Braithwaite & Sons Limited
Wolverhampton, England

© Michael J. Morgan 1986

ISBN 0 86023 311 1

Acknowledgements

I am grateful first and foremost to all those Bicester people who have given me old photographs over the years — after 1920 the bulk of the other pictures were taken by my father, William Harris Morgan, who started business in Bicester, on the Market Square, in 1920. I have had a lot of help from Peter Barrington, Chief Reporter on the *Bicester Advertiser*, especially from his cuttings library at the paper. Last but not least, I am in the debt of Bicester's past historians — men like White Kennett, John Dunkin, David Watts and especially Sid G. Hedges.

Barracuda Guide to County History Vol II Oxfordshire Geoffrey Stevenson MA, Barracuda Books Ltd, 1977

Bicester wuz a little town Sid Hedges (S.G.), 1968 *Bicester Advertiser*; reprinted 1974 Bicester Book Shop

The Bicester and Warden Hill A. S. Barrow, 1928

The Buildings of England: Oxfordshire J. Sherwood and N. Pevsner, Penguin, 1974

Concise Oxford Dictionary of English Place Names Eilert Ekwall, Oxford, (4th edition) 1960

The History and Antiquities of Bicester and the Hundreds of Bullingdon and Ploughly John Dunkin, 1823

History of the Deanery of Bicester J. C. Blomfield, 1882

Parochial Antiquities White Kennett, 1695

Paterson's Roads Edward Mogg, 1826

The Place-Names of Oxfordshire M. Gelling, 1944

Post Office Directory of Northamptonshire, Huntingdonshire, Bedfordshire, Buckinghamshire, Berkshire and Oxfordshire Kelly & Co, 1864 and 1887

A Short History of Bicester Priory D. J. Watts, 1983

Bicester is a child of communications — a crossroads originally born of military necessity. Any motorist driving across the Vale from Aylesbury soon senses he is on a Roman road — the straight-as-a-dye Akeman Street. In the middle ages, Bicester became a significant market centre for the surrounding farmland — all local roads led there. When the heyday of the coaches came, Bicester was a posting town, and the turnpikes made it more so. In the age of steam, not one but two railways linked the town with the LMS and the GWR networks. Early 20th century Bicester became a bigger cattle and sheep marketplace, and then the motorcar reached out to embrace it. Today the M40's influence is already felt — and in the skies above, space-age jets thunder to and from their local base. Each step along the way has enlarged the populace, until today Bicester is a thriving, growing, residential, commuter and service centre. Yet it all began nearly 2,000 years ago, with a civil engineering problem that flummoxed the Romans.

It was the latin legions that created Alchester in the middle of the first century AD, on low-lying marshland between the modern site of Bicester and the village of Wendlebury to the south. Alchester was just off the crossroads formed by Akeman Street — from Cirencester to Verulamium — and another (unnamed) road linking Dorchester and Towcester. Even today, Akeman Street still links Kirtlington and Chesterton, and forms the modern A41 from Bicester to Aylesbury.

But the Romans had a problem which bedevilled them everywhere they marched across The Vale. Excavations in the mid-1980s showed those great engineers of the past managed to raise their township two feet above original ground level, across a 26 acre site — but their drains still got blocked, and their watercourses silted up. For The Vale was then a myriad of streams crisscrossing a damp, uncultivated and untillable marshland. Roads driven across this inhospitable terrain were all causeways — like that which passed the trading post at Fleet Marston near the site of Aylesbury, built more sensibly on a Chiltern foothill.

When the Romans departed in the fifth century, their drainage works collapsed and the area reverted to marsh. Today Alchester is but a memory, unnoticed, unsignposted and unmarked on modern maps — just farmland. At the time, the native Celts, and presumably the later Saxons, had the good sense to shift their homes onto slightly higher ground, and thus Bicester was born.

By the time William and his Norman marauders landed, Bicester was a viable market town, and Domesday 1086 records exactly 900 years ago that *Bernecestre* had two mills, and was ruled by Robert d'Oilly, Sheriff of Oxfordshire and Warwickshire, and Constable of Oxford Castle. One of those watermills was near the present-day junction of Queen's Avenue (opened in 1939 on the line of the Alchester-Towcester Roman road) and St John's Street — on the Bure, or stream, that runs through the town centre. The other, also on the Bure, stood at the western end of Priory Road, close to the old London-Bicester turnpike, now Priory Lane.

The town's name itself has been variously attributed. Some ascribe it to Birinus, the saintly seventh century Saxon who legend says founded a frontier garrison by the ruins of Roman Alchester. Others cite the Saxon for granary (*bern*) and latin for town (*ceaster*) to reflect the marketplace. Variations are legion: Burencester, Birini-Castrum, Birincestre, Burincastre, and the 13th century Burnecestre, possibly echoing the Royal forest of Bernwood. But

Domesday's Bernecestre probably reflects the Old English terms *byrgen* and *ceaster* — burial mound and Roman fort; perhaps the higher ground was first used to bury Caesar's men, and later to build upon their bones.

Given a prosperous little vill, it was not surprising that in 1145 the nuns of Markyate established themselves here at Nonnes Place — the site of the later Coker home, Bicester House. But in 1182, Gilbert Bassett, heir to Milo de Crispin's Norman estates, established a Priory for eleven Black Canons. His foundation stood on the present day Old Place Yard and included a church larger than the neighbouring 12th century St Edburg's parish church outside its gates. Old Priory House in Priory Lane is believed to have been the Canons' guest house. The spiritual tendency continued when Alan Bassett founded a chantry at Bicester in 1243 so that two clerks could study at Oxford.

The Priory was short of teachers in 1520, visited by Henry VIII in 1526 and dissolved ten years later, the good Canons pensioned off. Elizabeth I stayed in the cloister buildings in 1568 while on a Midlands progress — three years short of four centuries later, Elizabeth II was in town too.

In 1656 the Priory estate and buildings were bought by John Glynne, who later became Chief Justice of the King's Bench but, on his death, the cloisters were demolished and his son William used the stone to build a mansion at Ambrosden, also since demolished. Apart from Old Priory House, only the dovecote and outbuildings survive — as part of St Edburg's Parish Centre in Old Place Yard.

The Parish Church itself, the competition eliminated, is now the most imposing building in the town, visible from almost every quarter, its 12th century bulk and graceful late Perpendicular tower a conspicuous landmark.

For the post-dissolution town, and right up to the late 19th century, control was divided. Indeed Bicester was two townships — King's End and Market End — each with their own overseers, guardians and churchwardens, though all within a single parish. The origin of this curious split apparently lay in the original grants of fairs and markets. In 1239 a market was granted to William de Longspee at Market End. In 1377 Richard II granted a three day fair at King's End.

Market End was enclosed in 1758 and King's End in 1794. In 1820 the Bicester hunt was formed; the town was both benefactor and beneficiary — 'Bicester owes much of its prosperity [to the Hunt] for which the country around is well adapted'. And in 1826 a national observer noted 'Bicester is a very neat town, containing several handsome residences, and the church is a spacious structure'. Within forty years 'the chief business of the inhabitants arises from their well attended markets and cattle fairs', and in 1887 it was 'an agricultural market town . . . [where] the air is healthy and the water pure, and to the use of it [is] attributed the celebrity the town has obtained for its excellent ale' (first brewed in 1846). In fact in 1864 the town boasted twenty inns apart from beershops.

With all this public provision, more aesthetic needs were not overlooked. In 1669 Samuel Blackwell opened a school and his assistant was White Kennett, who in 1686 became Ambrosden's vicar, ten years later publishing his *Parochial Antiquities* — Bicester's first history. Dissenting spirits were served by John Troughton in 1692, whose ministry was supported by Henry Cornish's barn services — in 1729 the Congregational Chapel was built, on a site cleared by fire.

Bicester indeed suffered a series of disasters at the time: in

1683 an earthquake struck, followed in 1704 by smallpox, and in 1718, 1724 and 1730 by fire, consuming many buildings in Water Lane — a 'sudden and terrible' outbreak (1724) — and in King's End (1730). In 1765 the Church itself caught fire, struck by lightning.

Yet the town's faith was undiminished, with the new Wesleyan Church in North Street in 1840, the United Free Methodist Church in Sheep Street in 1862, and the Catholic Church and school of 1883; eighty years later a new RC Church was opened in the Causeway.

Mind as well as spirit was the concern of James Jones in 1794, when he founded a Sunday School to teach the three Rs, but local protest soon cut him down to reading and Christian principles — principles that failed to prevent the illegitimate birthrate rising in 1799 from 28 to 79. Perhaps they should have let Mr Jones complete his good works? By 1836 the Workhouse had been opened — for 320 people.

Education came into its own by 1858, when the National Schools were founded for 400 children, and in 1872 the Reading Room was built, St Edburg's Hall following within a decade. Just as well, since in 1826 the 17th century Town Hall and the old butchers' Shambles were destroyed by a disorderly mob. Perhaps some of these were among the 85 paupers the Vestry sent packing to Liverpool *en route* to a new life in the New World in 1830. Certainly, in 1921 St Edburg's Hall was a contender for Town Hall status, but civic pride was still unsatisfied by 1964 when £100,000 housing fund surplus was set aside, plans only to be deferred three years later. Today a Civic Centre in the grounds of The Garth is under fierce debate — and undecided.

Less might have been achieved were it not for Bicester's increasing importance as a crossroads. The Bicester-Aylesbury turnpike, on the old Roman road, was established in 1770. By the next century the town was seen as on the 'old' mail route to Birmingham from London. Yet it had taken 25 years for the first mailcoach to leave for metropolis. Nonetheless, locals were industrious, blending market and communications to send ten tons of butter to London weekly in 1809. Coach travellers in the 1820s found Bicester entered as 'From Tyburn Turnpike to Aylesbury . . . Cross the river Thame, Waddesdon, Ham Green, Black Thorn Heath, Oxon, Bicester'. In 1877 the road was 'disturnpiked' for, 27 years earlier, the railways arrived, and two years later, in 1879, the LMS absorbed that first link, while in 1910 the GWR came to town. In 1968 passengers had to look to other means of travel, when the service was axed. Today only freight travels the Bletchley line, while passengers use Bicester North.

Although Pevsner remarked sniffily in 1974, 'There is little to see in Bicester, a small market town which, to judge by its buildings, has never been wealthy . . .' the town has its share of attractive properties. The three main surviving houses are Bicester House, The Garth and Bicester Hall.

Bicester House, whose walled garden fronts King's End and Queen's Avenue, gives the town a valuable green 'lung' in the centre, and has ancient origins. It was the manor house of the nuns of Markyate, from whom it was purchased by John Coker in 1584, and it remained in the Coker family until the late 1970s. The house seen today dates from the 17th century, was enlarged in 1780, but seriously damaged by fire shortly after. It has been much altered, and was re-modelled in 1820. The Coker family were Lords of the Manor of King's End and played a major part in the town's life.

The Garth in Launton Road is now the offices of Bicester

Town Council. It was a hunting lodge and owned by the Keith-Falconer family. During the 1939-45 war it was commandeered by the Army and afterwards Major Adrian Keith-Falconer wanted to sell up. However, a member of another local family, Major the Hon Arthur Child-Villiers, second son of the seventh Earl of Jersey of Middleton Park, Middleton Stoney, intervened.

Four benefactors bought it for £7,000, well below the market value, and presented it to the town in 1946. They were Major Keith-Falconer, Major Child-Villiers, Major Philip Fleming, whose family live at Barton Abbey, Middle Barton, and the then Lord Bicester.

Their benefaction is recorded by a plaque on a gate pillar to The Garth at the main Launton Road entrance. Land there has provided space for Bicester Bowls and Bicester Tennis Clubs to have their greens and courts, and the formal gardens are the only public parkland in the town. The Garth itself became the offices of the former Bicester Urban District Council and then the subsequent Town (parish) Council in 1974. In the gardens just inside the main gate is in the only surviving relic of The Shambles that used to stand in Market Square — the bell.

Bicester Hall stands on the corner of London Road and Launton Road and, after years of dereliction, was bought, improved and extended in 1985-86 to provide flats for the elderly. It dates from at least 1874, when it was the home of Baron William Henry John Shroeder and later, local physician, W. H. Davis. The Earl of Cottenham owned the house from at least 1896, when it was a hunting box. Bicester was second only to Melton Mowbray as a centre for hunting, and the Bicester and Warden Hill has remained one of the most fashionable hunts in the country. In 1986 it absorbed the Whaddon Chase, and is now called the Bicester Hunt with the Whaddon Chase, the kennels remaining at Stratton Audley, a few miles north of the town.

Bicester Hall was later owned by Mr Roland Hermon Hodge of Rousham and became a convalescent hospital in November 1914 for war wounded. In 1919 it was bought by Oxfordshire County Council and opened as Bicester County School in 1924. After 38 years the school moved to a new site at Highfields, where Bicester Secondary School had already been established. Two years later they amalgamated as Bicester Comprehensive School. While the main house became offices for the Department of Employment, the courtyard at the back became a youth and community centre; Bicester Day Centre for the elderly and needy was established there too, although by 1986 work was due to begin on a purpose-built day centre on the old garden or playground of Bicester Hall.

The town itself became a local government district in 1858 — with the establishment of the first two 'townships' — and in 1894 the Urban District Council was formed. Eighty years later it was no more, a successor Town Council the remnant of town organisation. If politicians come and go, the fourth estate somehow survives. In 1887 there were three newspapers — *Advertiser*, *Herald* and *Telegraph*, the first 'neutral' the other two in the Liberal interest. The *Advertiser*, which absorbed the *Herald*, is still with us today.

Gas beat the politicians' hot air by arriving as early as 1845; Bicester's darkness was not publicly lightened until the electric came in 1929; water was piped into the town in 1905. Moving pictures arrived in 1934 (the Regal, a bingo hall since the mid-'60s) and behind the Crown (gutted in 1943).

In the town centre, commerce has wrought several changes — in Sheep Street, Market Square and The Causeway. At one time a block of shops with homes above stood across Sheep Street at the southern end, but it was demolished to make way for road improvements.

Another victim of the demolition squads was the old Crown Hotel that became Tesco. Many criticised the stark appearance of the supermarket, but plans are now afoot to bring it down as part of a better designed shopping mall.

While Market Square has seen relatively few changes, The Causeway lost some of its more characterful buildings in 1972. Bridge House, and the Rose and Crown Inn stood at the Market Square end of The Causeway, where Manorsfield Road now begins, and where there is a modern block of shops, a bank and flats.

The Rose and Crown was reputed to be the oldest pub in Bicester, dating back to the 16th century. The proximity of the pub to Bridge House was fortuitous. For a time Bridge House was the offices and meeting place of Bicester Urban District Council and an oft-told tale was that a councillor would move a temporary adjournment of Council business just before the pub's closing time.

Bridge House was originally home to the manager of Hall's Oxford Brewery local branch. The brewery was in the yard at the back, and horse-drawn drays set out for town and village rounds. The yard also housed the mineral water works of North and Randall of Aylesbury, and their branch manager, George Timberlake, lived in a house there too.

After the Urban District Council moved out to The Garth, Bridge House became the Bicester branch of the County Library Service in May 1949. The Library stayed until shortly before demolition, and went to a new building in Old Place Yard. The yard of Bridge House became known as Corporation Yard, and for a time was home to fire brigade and ambulance services.

On open land off The Causeway was Bicester's open air swimming pool, constructed in the early 1930s. It was filled in and swimmers transferred their allegiance to the already opened indoor pool at Bicester and Ploughley Sports Centre.

Bicester has always been a sporting town, and has benefitted from the foresight of local people. In 1896 the town's football club was founded, and well before the 1939-45 war, land was acquired from the Coker family to establish the Bicester Sports Club beside the Oxford Road. It is administered by a trust and is completely self-sufficient.

In the last two decades Bicester has lost its Council, gained in population and seen much of its townscape demolished. Today it is once more the centre of communications for the surrounding countryside, and host to a multiple military and airborne presence, from the Central Ordnance Depôt to the Royal Corps of Transport 25 'Carmen' Freight Squadron, from the world-ranging jets of USAF Upper Heyford to the RAF Gliding and Soaring Association, who utilise the old Bicester aerodrome.

Once more many roads lead to Bicester — home to commuter, commerce and combat forces; a town of tradition, growth and some national significance.

View across the Market Square in 1860, from the Kings Arms corner. The main block of buildings in the centre remain the same, but 'Hedges Block' on the extreme right was demolished in 1963 for road widening purposes, enabling the A41 to run straight through the town.

From the London Road end of Market Hill, showing the Hedges block demolished in 1963. This was taken in 1925.

The central block of Market Square in 1890; the top storey of the square buildng on the left of the block had disappeared by 1908.

Bicester Market Square after an extremely heavy snow storm on 26 April 1908, clearly showing the so-called 'fountain', really a drinking place for people, horses, and dogs, shaped like a clover leaf.

LEFT: Bicester Hunt meet outside the Kings Arms Hotel in 1851; directly behind the hounds, the local 'bobby' with his stovepipe hat and shiny buckled belt. RIGHT: Traditional Boxing Day meet of the Bicester Hunt on the Market Square in 1909. The large shop and house in the background is Flemons the drapers, and it seems likely that this is where King Henry VIII stayed overnight when he passed through Bicester on 11 September 1526 on his way from Winchester to Ampthill in Beds.

An old print: the Shambles which stood on the Market Square until 1826. Originally animals were slaughtered and the meat sold there, but by about 1800 butchers were just selling the meat, the slaughtering done elsewhere at their own premises. The Shambles bell was saved and now stands in the grounds of the Garth Park, headquarters of the present Bicester Town Council.

The George Hotel stood on the George Corner, until replaced by the Midland Bank in 1920, with the original Bicester Post Office next to it. This was the entrance to the Square from Sheep Street at the turn of the century.

A very dilapidated print of Bicester Town Band from about 1880. Top hats and smocks appear to be the uniform.

Bicester Sheep Fair on the Market Square in 1905; held for many decades, first in the streets, and then Market Square, when pens were built in Sheep Street and along most of Kings End. Around 1910 the fair moved to a field next to Bardwell Terrace up Bell Lane, where it remained until 1959, when it moved to the edge of town in a field on Buckingham Road, between Bicester and the RAF airfield. In the lat 1970s this site was required for building and it moved to part of the airfield at nearby Finmere, where it is held at present, one of the largest sheep fairs in the country.

Celebrating the accession of King Edward VII in 1901 by striking volleys on four anvils outside the smith and farriers' forge on the Market Square. The anvils had holes in their upper sides, and black powder was rammed in with a wooden wedge. Then a heated iron was pushed through a smaller hole in the anvil's side and the powder exploded, sending the wedge high into the air, all the children hoping to catch it. Sirett's is now Lissetter's antique shop, and Withey next door is Bucknell and Ballard. Hedges in the corner is an Indian restaurant.

18

Crowds gather on the Square to celebrate the Coronation of George V and Queen Mary in June 1911. The shops on the left are still the same, except for some modern fronts; Bates, later Lewis' and then Boot's was a chemists, Harris the jewellers became the Electricity Board showrooms. Next to them Scrivener's Haberdashery is now a freezer centre; the next shop, once the Black Boy, is now Wadley's television and radio; next, Bowne's the hairdresser and then Ambrosden House, which is now a shop, but started originally as the Swan Inn. On the right the Rose and Crown and the large Bridge House next to it have disappeared to make way for Manorsfield Road, providing an alternative route up to St John's Street, avoiding the town centre.

Staff of Bicester Post Office in 1900 with Postmaster Walter French between the two ladies. The Post Office was on Market Square, next to the George Hotel, until the present one was built in Sheep Street. The building is now Sketchley dry cleaners.

The Bicester YMCA Band pictured on the Market Square at the turn of the century; one of Bicester's most successful, folding-up just before the first world war. The bandmaster was Mr William Grimsley, an accomplished musician, who was killed in the war. The band met and practised in the Causeway, where the YMCA had a gymnasium, billiard room, and bandroom.

In July 1931, Bicester held an Empire Shopping Week, and here, Councillor Tom Hudson, the Chairman of the Executive Committee, leads the Fancy Dress Parade through the Market Square, dressed as a Hussar.

Stuchfield the Saddler stood at No 24 Market Square, and was run for some years by Mrs Elizabeth Stuchfield, pictured here with her children John, Mary, Agnes and Kate, after the death of her husband John. Elizabeth died in 1912, and the business was then run for a good many years by son John, until it was sold to Mr & Mrs Walt Dagley, who ran a dairy and café. Next it became the Bicester branch of the NatWest Bank, and is undergoing yet another change at the moment.

Bicester Scout band, drums and bugles, lead the troop through the Market Square on a St George's Day parade in the 1920s.

A later view of the north side of the Square in the mid-thirties, when cars were rather thinner on the ground, and bicycle racks were provided for the many 'cyclists from the surrounding villages.

Another print from the 1931 Empire Shopping Week held in Bicester in July, this time showing proud mums and bonny babies who were successful in the Baby Show.

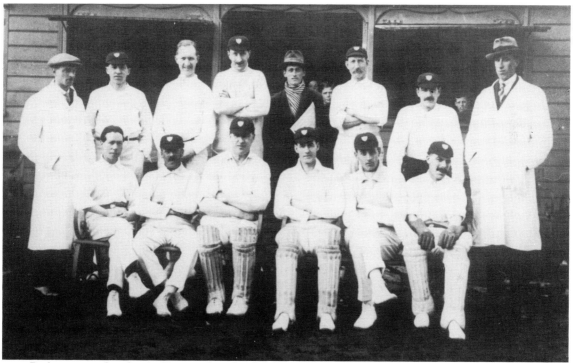

Businessmen and traders in Bicester who enjoyed their sport, but could not play on Saturday, formed a Thursday Cricket XI, Thursday being half day closing: in front of the old, long-gone cricket pavilion at Bicester Sports Ground standing left to right: Haynes, Ingram, G. Sibbring, W. Harris-Morgan (author's father), E. Roderick, G. Lapper, A. Whetton, Ponsford; sitting: A. Stanley, Merritt, Bustin, G. Southern, A. V. Bowne, J. Brain. Photographed during the 1925 season.

An outing to Stratford-on-Avon organised by Mr H. Bustin, landlord of the Red Lion Inn on the Market Square, in an Oxford charabanc in July 1922 or 1923. The people in the photograph from left to right are: F. Haynes, H. Bustin, W. Haynes, T. Buckland, H. Hazell, W. Waite, F. Hawtin, G. Dean, L. Turney, H. Hawtin, S. Palmer, J. Coggins,, W. Grace, F. Neal, H. Mouring, H. Smith, T. Richardson, G. Grace, G. Dancer, R. Neal, S. Coggins, F. Massey, R. Clifton, W. Massey, and E. Hall. G. Dancer Senior is standing by the charabanc; and the landlady, Mrs Bustin, and her sister are looking out of the Red Lion window.

The only way to travel; this is how mail and parcel post were delivered to village post offices at the turn of the century and up to the first world war. Mr Harry Hornsby, a well known postman of the time, is about to set out on his rounds.

LEFT: The forge at 17 Market Square, by now owned by 'Jagger the Vet'; standing outside from left to right are Bert Bourton (holding the horse), Fred Smith (the blacksmith), Jessie Smith, and Will Pitts. The narrow alley behind the horse led up the yard to the smithy and several stables. RIGHT: Early 1920s Market Square shop: Lambourn's 'cycle shop, now Visionhire TV Rental. Jim Coles on the left, a mechanic in the bicycle workshop at the rear, chats to a customer, while the poster in the window offers a 'first class cycle' for a season's hire at £2 10s 0d (£2.50). The shop was also an agency for Wheeler and Wilson's sewing machines. Oliver Cromwell slept in the room above the archway, when his forces were marching to attack the Royalists at Claydon in 1644.

Running from the Market Square westwards to the parish church of St Edburg's is a narrow street called The Causeway, and here at No 5, now the offices of the Bicester Advertiser, Mary and William Smith stand outside their grocer shop, decorated to celebrate Queen Victoria's Diamond Jubilee of 1897. The cottage next door is now a Chinese restaurant, but was then a blacksmithy belonging to T. Sirett, who later moved up to the northern side of the Market Square.

LEFT: Bicester's narrowest street, The Causeway, in 1909. The cottages on the left of the picture are no longer there; Thomas Grimsley had his builder's yard behind, later to become Harry Bonner's stables. This was then demolished and the Roman Catholic Church built in 1962. The music shop on the extreme right became a house for many years but is back as a shop now, dealing in antiques. RIGHT: The Causeway, as its name implies, crosses the town stream, the Bure, and in the early part of the century would flood after a particularly heavy rain; this photo shows the baker delivering his bread on horseback, by passing it through the upstairs windows, before the first world war.

The Causeway from the Church between the wars, looking much as it does at the present time, except for the building on the extreme left having been demolished, and the large building, Bridge House, just visible at the far end on the left also gone, to make way for the new Manorsfield link road.

In 1933 a swimming pool was built in Bicester behind Bridge House in The Causeway, partly to give jobs to the unemployed during the Depression, and also to give the children somewhere to swim. A committee was set up, some of whom can be seen here during construction. In the centre, with his foot on a piece of timber is Mr Albert Lambourne, chairman of the committee; to his left is Mr Morley Smith, baker and councillor; further left Mr H. T. Smith, council surveyor stands between two workmen. To the right of Mr Lambourne is Mr J. T. Mountain, chemist, wearing a topcoat, and third from right is Mr J. L. Howson, headmaster of Bicester County School. The pool was in use until the modern Bicester and Ploughley Sports Centre complex was built.

The remnants of Bicester Priory: Old Place Yard, (now the home of Major Moir), showing the dovecote on the left. The site now contains the County Library, St Edburg's old folks' home, and old people's bungalows, as well as the Social Services offices, which were all built in the mid-1960s.

Print of the Parish Church of St Edburg, dated 1849.

The interior of the Parish Church in 1840, and as it was until 1863, when it was changed at a cost of £3,214. The galleries were removed; so was the ancient wooden chancel screen. The whole Church was reseated to provide for 1,050 persons, new choir stalls provided, and a new stone and marble pulpit. A new iron chancel screen was erected, but was removed in 1896. A large part of the roofing was also replaced.

1885 view of the Church with the vicarage directly in front, from the Kings End side. The two public houses are still the same; the Six Bells and, nearer the camera the Swan; apart from road surfacing and yellow lines the view is the same today.

Tennis on the Vicarage lawn in 1885, for the Vicar, Rev Blackburne-Kane and his family. This large Vicarage, situated right next to the Parish Church, is now a private residence, and a much smaller and more modest Vicarage was built in Victoria Road in the 1970s.

Bicester Church School at the turn of the century; the building has not altered, and is now St Edburg's Primary School, but this view can no longer be seen because of modern classrooms built in the foreground.

William Piggott, Headmaster of the Church School on 8 September 1923 officially opened Bicester's new Sports Ground by kicking the first ball. The sports ground was previously called Barn Piece, and golf was played there.

Opposite the Six Bells in Church Street stood a wheelwright's and coachbuilder, founded in 1810 by a Mr William Townsend, but in 1923 taken over by Mr John Hollis. The picture shows the premises in 1925 with Mr Hollis, his son John (left), and younger brother Bob, and also their cousin Florrie. Iron tyres for Oxfordshire wagons were put on in the workshops, while the upholstery for carriages was done upstairs. The paintshop was at the back and, when finished, the vehicles were brought out into the street and the shafts fitted with the help of an artificial horse.

Looking north up Kings End from the Oxford Road at the turn of the century, one was faced with the main entrance to Bicester House, where the road turned sharp right into Church Street and the town centre. About 1938, Queens Avenue was built from the corner across 'the fields' (up to then just a footpath), to the junction of Field Street, and St John's Street, and the entrance to the house was moved down opposite Home Farm.

Bicester Nursing Home, pictured in 1912, and standing back from the Oxford road in Kings End. Built in 1908, the Nursing Home was added to over the years, became the Cottage Hospital, maternity hospital, and finally is now known as Bicester Community Hospital.

Kings End about 1930, looking south towards the Oxford Road. The straight eight mile Bicester-Kidlington stretch was not built till 1938, and the journey was a winding one through several villages. The houses on the right beyond the second telephone pole have all been demolished, making way for a large garage on the site of Parrot's Garage, and the Kings Avenue road onto the 'Western Development' housing estate built in the 1950s.

The Kings End section of the Bicester Sheep Fair in 1909, in front of the old Manor House. The lone lime tree in the centre of the picture is the 'Hallelujah Tree', under which the Salvation Army, with its band, used to hold services.

The eastern end of the Market Square has two exits, the Square actually being triangular; here the southernmost one joins the London Road at the Kings Arms corner. Claremont House, (left with railings), was then home to Mr T. C. Finch, whose high-class grocery shop was next door. Next was Dean's the ironmongers, recently closed, and then the home of Dr Holmes. At the side of the Kings Arms, just behind the young cyclist, is one of John Dearn's old taxis; he ran his business from a garage behind the hotel.

Fancy dressers celebrating the 1911 coronation of George V, outside Claremont House. The joke advert 'Try Jegger's Petrol Food for Hosses' would seem to refer to the increasing number of internal combustion vehicles appearing on the streets.

Three of Bicester's hostelries in a row, two of them now defunct, pictured in 1885. The imposing frontage of the Kings Arms has not changed; behind it, the Nag's Head, and behind yet again the Kings Head, are both no longer separate pubs, but all part of the Kings Arms Hotel.

Looking up the London Road from the Launton Road corner, the Kings Arms Arms Hotel on the left, the imposing building on the right is Bicester Hall. Here in the 1920s it was Bicester County School. The Hall dates from the 1870s, when it was the residence of Baron William Shroeder. The Earl of Cottenham enlarged it and added stabling; it became a hospital for war wounded in 1914 and Bicester County School in 1924. In 1946, it changed to Bicester Grammar School and finally closed in the early 1960s.

Staff and pupils of Bicester County School at the end of the first year, in July 1925, with Headmaster John Howson and his three staff members in the centre front. The school finally closed in 1964, when it joined Bicester Secondary School to become Bicester Comprehensive School.

Further down London Road on the same side as Bicester Hall is the Hermitage (1906), and the signboard up on the front wall is a trade sign for 'Gent' Baker, an undertaker, so called because of his tall build, and because he always wore a bowler. The railings on the extreme right are those of Rose Cottage, and the entrance between the two runs into the Garth Park. All the buildings on the left of the road have now been demolished, the road widened, and a mini-roundabout installed.

Looking southwards down the London Road from Rose Cottage, the new St Edburg's Hall, built in 1882, dominates the view in 1885. There were no houses beyond, except the stationmaster's house near the railway. Priory Road, which now runs this side of the Hall, was still some years away.

The old Claypits, complete with swans, pictured in the 1920s. Clay dug here was made into bricks in the adjoining 'brick field'. Boating, fishing and, in the winter, skating, were all popular here, but in the late '20s the Council decided to fill them in, refuse tipping began and the site is now an Oxford County Highways depôt.

Bicester Fire Brigade, complete with horse-drawn steamer Princess May, in the stableyard of Bicester Hall in 1923; back: Fmn J. Hollis, R. Trinder, T. Pilbeam; second row: Fmn T. Hill, and C. Box; standing: Fmn A. Pinchin, Engnr G. Aldridge, Fmn A. H. Simmonds, Asst Engnr E. A. Clifton, 1st Officer H. T. Smith, Hon Sec F. Hudson, 2nd Officer J. W. Knibb, Fmn J. Gostlow and A. Fleet.

The George Corner in 1900, where the northern exit from the Market Square joins Sheep Street, the main street. The George was demolished to build the Midland Bank in 1920; next to it is Truman's, solicitor, then came 'Fishy' Grimsley's fish shop, now a shoe shop; the next two buildings have been demolished. A branch of the Trustee Savings Bank now stands where Messenger's, auctioneers, were and Tesco built a supermarket on the site of the Crown Hotel.

View of Bicester cattle market in Sheep Street, taken from an upper window in the Market Hill block in September 1908.

Looking down the southern part of Sheep Street in 1909, the main difference is the large Market Hill block, missing at the end of the Street, and the roadway going straight through to continue on the London Road. The large house on the left is Lloyd's Bank. Palmer Bros, the ironmonger's next door, became Ashmore's, burnt down in 1969 and rebuilt. The White Hart is next and has not changed, but the next two premises belonging to Goble's have been demolished and rebuilt as one modern shop, where Mike Goble carries on a long family tradition as florist and greengrocer.

George Corner on 4 July 1915, when the bottom end of Sheep Street flooded after a heavy rainstorm. Mr George Goble, whose shop can be seen on the left, waded out to see if the drains were blocked, and Council Surveyor Mr Pearson, with the stick, joined him.

How long would it take the staff of Hilton's Booteries to set out this display, and take it in again at night? Most of the boots and shoes appear to be well under ten shillings (fifty-pence) per pair and, judging by that, and the three large gas lamps along the front, the photograph must date from the early years of the century.

The eastern side of lower Sheep Street from the George Corner, shows another of Bicester's long closed pubs, the Bear, third from the right. Around 1900 Mr Tom Druce bought the building and added it to his drapery shop at London House next door, (the shop with the blinds). Later in the '20s it was taken over as a separate shop again by Mr Grimes as a men's outfitter, and is now a furniture shop.

In the winter of 1916 a fire broke out in the roof of Mr Tom Druce's shop, and lit up the whole street. According to contemporary reports, Mrs Percy Harris, who lived there, raised the alarm about midnight, and the firemen were hampered by cold winds, and freezing water. Bicester fire chief Timberlake can be seen by the foot of the ladder in the centre.

LEFT: Sandiland's the chemist when it was owned by RIGHT: Mr Robert Burgess Sandiland, who founded the business in 1832. It stayed with the family until taken over by Mr J. T. Mountain in 1902. It was run by Mr Mountain and his daughter Dorothy, who carried on after her father's death, until she retired in the 1960s. The building was then sold and demolished, and a supermarket built for Fine Fare. To the right is a large private house that became a fruit shop and a café after the war, was also demolished in the '60s and became the site for Woolworth.

The Crown Hotel in Sheep Street was demolished in 1963 to allow a Tesco supermarket to be built — it is itself under threat of demolition for a new shopping mall.

Alf Evans, ladies and gents outfitters and drapers, started business in 1902 in Sheep Street. Pictured here in 1906 are Alf, on the right of the archway, his wife Nellie on the left, and son John between them. Mr Evans moved across Sheep Street in 1917 to much larger premises, and the two shops shown here were split up once more. The yard is still Evans' yard, and is now an arcade of some six small shops.

This row of three thatched cottages, halfway up Sheep Street on the western side, pictured around the first world war, stood like this until the late '20s, when the thatch caught fire. The cottages (the end one on the left was in fact a butcher's shop belonging to Arthur Grace) were evacuated, the furniture and the meat from the butcher's stacked in the newly built Methodist Church opposite. The cottages were re-roofed with slate.

This is the fire that destroyed the thatched roofs of the row of cottages including Grace the butcher. In the foreground can be seen the furniture and personal possessions of the householders stacked in the front garden of the newly erected Methodist Church.

The northern end of Sheep Street up to the junction with St John's Street, in 1908. The building on the extreme left of the picture is the Reading Room, provided by the Earl of Jersey of Middleton Park, for 'working men', and it is now Peter Judd's grocery shop; next is the Wesley Hall, home then of the Methodist Sunday School, now a furniture shop; then two more shops lie either side of Wesley Yard, itself today a shopping precinct.

Right on the corner of Sheep Street and St John's Street stood the Star public house, seen here with landlord Alf Clifton, not long before it closed in 1936 and the licence was transferred to the newly built replacement Star up the Bucknell Road, on the new Highfield estate. Mr Clifton also transferred to the new pub and retired after the war in 1947. This building was demolished in 1967, making way for the Franklins Yard car park.

Looking down North Street, the continuation of Sheep Street, in 1930. The cottage on the left, with the Aylesbury road sign, was demolished long ago; the next one is now a shop, and all the buildings on the right were demolished in 1979. The site is now occupied by blocks of flats, and the road has been widened.

View northward up North Street to the Top o' the Town, where North Street meets Field Street, the Banbury Road, and the Buckingham Road. This picture, taken in 1912, shows the old cottages on the right, which have all been demolished, making way for more flats, while the left hand side is still all standing.

Slightly lower down North Street in January 1937 where a tollgate stood in the middle of the last century, can be seen the cottages known as 'New Buildings'. These were built after a fire in 1724 burnt down many cottages in Water Lane, at the southern end of the town, where the Congregational Church (now a snooker hall), was built. The cottages up to the white shop with the bow window were demolished after the second world war, and the site is now an office block, and paved rest area known as 'Tollgate Seats'.

LEFT: 'Top o' the Town', the junction at the northern end of Bicester where the Buckingham, Banbury roads meet with North Street and Field Street. This old pump stood where the pavement is now, running down the Buckingham Road, and turning back on itself up the Banbury Road. The cottages behind are still in existence. RIGHT: Bicester's last windmill; it stood at the junction of the Middleton and Bignell (Chesterton) Roads, and was destroyed in 1886.

Buckingham Road in the mid '20s, looking from the GWR embankment south, towards the Top o' the Town junction. The recently built council houses can be picked out, sparkling white, and the empty space in the foreground is now completely built up.

George Street, on the new Highfield Council Estate in the 1920s; Orchard Cottage on the left, home of Nellie Hayes, standing on its own as the name suggests in a large orchard. This is now completely built up, the road running by the house is named Orchard Way, and it goes right through, to join up with Kings End estate.

The row of cottages at the end of St John's Street, where it turns right into Field Street, was demolished when Queens Avenue was built in 1938, to run left from the corner to Kings End corner and the Oxford Road, thereby avoiding the town centre.

Running from Sheep Street alongside the Bell to Victoria Road and Bardwell is Bell Lane. It was quite narrow and, in the late '50s, this facing cottage and the complete row running down to Sheep Street, visible at the far end, were demolished to allow it to be widened.

All these cottages were demolished in the early 1920s to allow the building of the Bicester Methodist Church (Grainger Hargreaves Memorial), in 1926/27. There were other cottages behind them, also demolished, whose entry was through Will's Yard, the first door on the left. Note the advertising plate for Hilton's Boots and Shoes, although their shop was farther down Sheep Street near the Square.

John Dunkin, Bicester's historian, lived in this cottage, which dates from 1699. Born in 1782, the son of a shoemaker, Dunkin published his History of Bicester in 1816, when he was 34 years old. He died in 1846, and the site of his cottage is now Dunkin's Close, a group of old people's bungalows.

Index to Illustrations

Market Square 1920s .... COVER
Market Square 1860 9
Market Hill 1925 10
Market Square 1890 11
Market Square 1908 12
Bicester Hunt 1851/1909 13
The Shambles 14
The George Corner 15
Bicester Town Band 1880 16
The Sheep Fair 1905 17
Anvil volleys for Edward VII 18
George V coronation crowds 19
Post Office staff 1900 20
YMCA Band c1900 21
Empire Shopping Week 1931 22
Stuchfield the saddler 23
Scout Band 1920s 24
Market Square 1930s 25
1931 Baby Show 26
Thursday Cricket XI 1925 27
Red Lion outing 1922/3 28
Horse mails 29
Jagger's forge 30
Lambourn's 'cycles 30
The Causeway 1897 31

The Causeway 1909 32
Floods in The Causeway 32
The Causeway 33
Swimming pool 1933 34
Old Place Yard 35
St Edburg Parish Church 1849 36
Inside St Edburg's 1840 37
Church and Vicarage 1885 38
Ecclesiastical tennis 1885 39
Bicester Church School 40
Barn Piece sports ground 1923 41
Hollis, coachbuilder, 1925 42
Kings End c1900 43
Bicester Nursing Home 1912 44
Kings End c1930 45
Sheep Fair 1909 46
Kings Arms Corner 47
Claremont House 1911 48
Kings Head, Nag's Head 1885 49
Bicester Hall 1920s 50
County School staff 1925 51
London Road 1906 52
St Edburg's Hall 1885 53
Claypits and swans 1920s 54
Fire Brigade 1923 55

The George Corner 1900 56
Bicester Cattle Market 1908 57
Sheep Street 1909 58
Floods of July 1915 59
Hilton's Booteries 60
Lower Sheep Street 61
1916 fire, Druce & Co 62
Sandiland's chemists 63
Robert Burgess Sandiland 63
Crown Hotel 64
Alf Evans 1906 65
Sheep Street cottages 66
1920s fire at Grace's 67
St John's and Sheep Streets 1908 68
The Star 1936 69
North Street 1930 70
Top o' the Town 71
Site of the tollgate 72
The old pump 73
The windmill 73
Buckingham Road 1920s 74
George Street 1920s 75
St John Street cottages 76
Bell Lane 77
Will's Yard 1920s 78
Dunkin's Cottage 79